The 3 Year Journal

for Teachers

Lisa McGrath

Oliver Golden Publishing

January 1

What are your intentions for this new year?

20_____

_____

_____

_____

_____

20_____

_____

_____

_____

_____

20_____

_____

_____

_____

_____

January 2

What did you learn in the last year?

20_____

_____

_____

_____

_____

20_____

_____

_____

_____

_____

20_____

_____

_____

_____

_____

January 3

Why did you become a teacher?

20_____

_____

_____

_____

_____

20_____

_____

_____

_____

_____

20_____

_____

_____

_____

_____

January 4

What district do you work in?

20_____

_____

_____

_____

_____

20_____

_____

_____

_____

_____

20_____

_____

_____

_____

_____

January 5

What grade do you teach?

20_____

_____

_____

_____

_____

20_____

_____

_____

_____

_____

20_____

_____

_____

_____

_____

January 6

What was your favorite subject in school?

20_____

_____

_____

_____

_____

20_____

_____

_____

_____

_____

20_____

_____

_____

_____

_____

January 7

How many students/classes do you teach?

20_____

_____

_____

_____

_____

20_____

_____

_____

_____

_____

20_____

_____

_____

_____

_____

January 8

What makes you smile?

20_____

_____

_____

_____

_____

20_____

_____

_____

_____

_____

20_____

_____

_____

_____

_____

January 9

What is your favorite book to teach?

20_____

_____

_____

_____

_____

20_____

_____

_____

_____

_____

20_____

_____

_____

_____

_____

January 10

What did you create today?

20_____

_____

_____

_____

_____

20_____

_____

_____

_____

_____

20_____

_____

_____

_____

_____

January 11

What is your philosophy of teaching?

20_____

_____

_____

_____

_____

20_____

_____

_____

_____

_____

20_____

_____

_____

_____

_____

January 12

What is present in your job that is fulfilling and full of potential?

20_____

_____

_____

_____

20_____

_____

_____

_____

20_____

_____

_____

_____

January 13

What advice would you give to a new teacher?

20_____

_____

_____

_____

_____

20_____

_____

_____

_____

_____

20_____

_____

_____

_____

_____

January 14

How important are career achievements to you?

20_____

_____

_____

_____

_____

20_____

_____

_____

_____

_____

20_____

_____

_____

_____

_____

January 15

What has been your biggest challenge in teaching?

20_____

_____

_____

_____

_____

20_____

_____

_____

_____

_____

20_____

_____

_____

_____

_____

January 16

What additional duties are assigned to you?

20_____

_____

_____

_____

_____

20_____

_____

_____

_____

_____

20_____

_____

_____

_____

_____

January 17

What is the most satisfying thing about teaching?

20_____

_____

_____

_____

_____

20_____

_____

_____

_____

20_____

_____

_____

_____

January 18

How much do you currently enjoy life outside of work or study?

20_____

_____

_____

_____

_____

20_____

_____

_____

_____

_____

20_____

_____

_____

_____

_____

January 19

How important is having a cleared off desk at the end of the day to you?

20_____

_____

_____

_____

20_____

_____

_____

_____

20_____

_____

_____

_____

January 20

What was the best part of today?

20_____

_____

_____

_____

_____

20_____

_____

_____

_____

_____

20_____

_____

_____

_____

_____

January 21

How do you encourage your students?

20_____

_____

_____

_____

_____

20_____

_____

_____

_____

_____

20_____

_____

_____

_____

_____

January 22

What is the scariest thing about teaching?

20_____

_____

_____

_____

20_____

_____

_____

_____

20_____

_____

_____

_____

January 23

How would your students describe you?

20_____

_____

_____

_____

_____

20_____

_____

_____

_____

_____

20_____

_____

_____

_____

January 24

What can you do for hours on end and often lose track of time?

20_____

_____

_____

_____

20_____

_____

_____

_____

20_____

_____

_____

_____

January 25

Are your current efforts going to help you achieve better life balance? If not, what needs to change?

20_____

_____

_____

_____

20_____

_____

_____

_____

20_____

_____

_____

_____

January 26

Define what 'success' means to you.

20_____

_____

_____

_____

_____

20_____

_____

_____

_____

_____

20_____

_____

_____

_____

_____

January 27

What are the important aspects of a good principal?

20_____

_____

_____

_____

_____

20_____

_____

_____

_____

_____

20_____

_____

_____

_____

_____

January 28

What did you learn about yourself in the last year?

20_____

_____

_____

_____

_____

20_____

_____

_____

_____

_____

20_____

_____

_____

_____

_____

January 29

Are you interested in extracurricular involvement?

20_____

_____

_____

_____

_____

20_____

_____

_____

_____

_____

20_____

_____

_____

_____

_____

January 30

Has anyone had a major impact on your life in the last year? How?

20_____

_____

_____

_____

20_____

_____

_____

_____

20_____

_____

_____

_____

_____

January 31

What is your least favorite subject to teach?

20_____

_____

_____

_____

_____

20_____

_____

_____

_____

_____

20_____

_____

_____

_____

_____

February 1

What is the difference between a good teacher and an exceptional teacher?

20_____

_____

_____

_____

_____

20_____

_____

_____

_____

_____

20_____

_____

_____

_____

_____

February 2

Have you ever been a substitute teacher?

20_____

_____

_____

_____

_____

20_____

_____

_____

_____

_____

20_____

_____

_____

_____

_____

February 3

What separates you from other teachers?

20_____

_____

_____

_____

_____

20_____

_____

_____

_____

_____

20_____

_____

_____

_____

_____

February 4

Describe your student teaching experience.

20_____

_____

_____

_____

20_____

_____

_____

_____

20_____

_____

_____

_____

February 5

What type of student were you in high school?

20_____

_____

_____

_____

_____

20_____

_____

_____

_____

_____

20_____

_____

_____

_____

_____

February 6

What activities and commitments have you made that don't suit you?

20_____

_____

_____

_____

_____

20_____

_____

_____

_____

_____

20_____

_____

_____

_____

_____

February 7

Are you currently active in any community service?

20_____

_____

_____

_____

_____

20_____

_____

_____

_____

_____

20_____

_____

_____

_____

_____

February 8

Do you want students to like you? Why or why not?

20_____

_____

_____

_____

_____

20_____

_____

_____

_____

_____

20_____

_____

_____

_____

_____

February 9

What behaviors are out of alignment with your personal and professional goals?

20_____

_____

_____

_____

20_____

_____

_____

_____

20_____

_____

_____

_____

February 10

What would your last boss say about you?

20_____

_____

_____

_____

_____

20_____

_____

_____

_____

_____

20_____

_____

_____

_____

_____

February 11

What do you need to give up complaining about?

20_____

_____

_____

_____

_____

20_____

_____

_____

_____

_____

20_____

_____

_____

_____

_____

February 12

What type of in-service topics are you most interested in?

20_____

_____

_____

_____

20_____

_____

_____

_____

20_____

_____

_____

_____

February 13

You get more of whatever you focus on: what are you focusing on?

20_____

_____

_____

_____

_____

20_____

_____

_____

_____

_____

20_____

_____

_____

_____

_____

February 14

What lesson has been a major success for your students?

20_____

_____

_____

_____

20_____

_____

_____

_____

20_____

_____

_____

_____

February 15

Do you belong to any professional organizations?

20_____

_____

_____

_____

_____

20_____

_____

_____

_____

_____

20_____

_____

_____

_____

_____

February 16

Is there anything that you are currently procrastinating on getting done?

20_____

_____

_____

_____

_____

20_____

_____

_____

_____

_____

20_____

_____

_____

_____

_____

February 17

Have you ever been in the newspaper?

20_____

_____

_____

_____

20_____

_____

_____

_____

20_____

_____

_____

_____

February 18

Are you a list maker and a planner?

20_____

_____

_____

_____

_____

20_____

_____

_____

_____

_____

20_____

_____

_____

_____

_____

February 19

Do you have a morning routine?

20_____

_____

_____

_____

_____

20_____

_____

_____

_____

_____

20_____

_____

_____

_____

_____

February 20

Do you have a weekly and/or monthly lesson plan?

20_____

_____

_____

_____

_____

20_____

_____

_____

_____

_____

20_____

_____

_____

_____

_____

February 21

Imagine you are at your retirement party at the end of your career. How would people describe you as a teacher?

20_____

_____

_____

_____

_____

20_____

_____

_____

_____

_____

20_____

_____

_____

_____

_____

February 22

Do a random act of kindness today. What did you do?

20_____

_____

_____

_____

_____

20_____

_____

_____

_____

_____

20_____

_____

_____

_____

_____

February 23

What are your top three strengths?

20_____

_____

_____

_____

_____

20_____

_____

_____

_____

20_____

_____

_____

_____

_____

February 24

Have you ever received an award?

20_____

_____

_____

_____

_____

20_____

_____

_____

_____

_____

20_____

_____

_____

_____

_____

February 25

How much time do you spend on lesson planning?

20_____

_____

_____

_____

_____

20_____

_____

_____

_____

_____

20_____

_____

_____

_____

_____

February 26

Do you take work home?

20_____

_____

_____

_____

_____

20_____

_____

_____

_____

_____

20_____

_____

_____

_____

_____

February 27

Are you able to do things that you enjoy frequently?

20_____

_____

_____

_____

_____

20_____

_____

_____

_____

_____

20_____

_____

_____

_____

_____

February 28

What has been one of the most difficult lessons you've learned?

20_____

_____

_____

_____

20_____

_____

_____

_____

20_____

_____

_____

_____

February 29

What are your interests outside of teaching?

20_____

_____

_____

_____

_____

20_____

_____

_____

_____

_____

20_____

_____

_____

_____

_____

February 30

Do you remember your favorite teacher?

20_____

_____

_____

_____

_____

20_____

_____

_____

_____

_____

20_____

_____

_____

_____

_____

March 1

Do you find contentment and fulfillment in your current career?

20_____

_____

_____

_____

20_____

_____

_____

_____

20_____

_____

_____

_____

March 2

Are you a flexible person?

20_____

_____

_____

_____

_____

20_____

_____

_____

_____

_____

20_____

_____

_____

_____

_____

March 3

Would you say you are a tough teacher?

20_____

_____

_____

_____

_____

20_____

_____

_____

_____

_____

20_____

_____

_____

_____

_____

March 4

What activities do you enjoy when you have free time?

20_____

_____

_____

_____

_____

20_____

_____

_____

_____

_____

20_____

_____

_____

_____

_____

March 5

What are your grading policies? Do you except late work?

20_____

_____

_____

_____

20_____

_____

_____

_____

20_____

_____

_____

_____

March 6

Do you make learning fun?

20_____

_____

_____

_____

_____

20_____

_____

_____

_____

_____

20_____

_____

_____

_____

_____

March 7

How well do you communicate your ideas to others?

20_____

_____

_____

_____

_____

20_____

_____

_____

_____

_____

20_____

_____

_____

_____

_____

March 8

Name five things you can do to work toward a larger goal
you have.

20_____

_____

_____

_____

20_____

_____

_____

_____

20_____

_____

_____

_____

March 9

What would you like to improve in your classroom?

20_____

_____

_____

_____

_____

20_____

_____

_____

_____

_____

20_____

_____

_____

_____

_____

March 10

What are you grateful for today?

20_____

_____

_____

_____

_____

20_____

_____

_____

_____

_____

20_____

_____

_____

_____

March 11

Who are the other teachers in your department?

20_____

_____

_____

_____

20_____

_____

_____

_____

20_____

_____

_____

_____

March 12

What is the best advice a principal gave you?

20_____

_____

_____

_____

_____

20_____

_____

_____

_____

_____

20_____

_____

_____

_____

_____

March 13

How do you integrate technology into your lessons?

20_____

_____

_____

_____

_____

20_____

_____

_____

_____

_____

20_____

_____

_____

_____

_____

March 14

What is a great mistake you have made, and why?

20_____

_____

_____

_____

_____

20_____

_____

_____

_____

_____

20_____

_____

_____

_____

_____

March 15

Are you a people pleaser?

20_____

_____

_____

_____

_____

20_____

_____

_____

_____

_____

20_____

_____

_____

_____

_____

March 16

How do you stay current in your field?

20_____

_____

_____

_____

_____

20_____

_____

_____

_____

_____

20_____

_____

_____

_____

_____

March 17

Is it okay for your classroom to be noisy?

20_____

_____

_____

_____

_____

20_____

_____

_____

_____

20_____

_____

_____

_____

March 18

Think about compliments people have given you. What was your favorite one and why?

20_____

_____

_____

_____

_____

20_____

_____

_____

_____

_____

20_____

_____

_____

_____

_____

March 19

How do you plan your curriculum units?

20_____

_____

_____

_____

_____

20_____

_____

_____

_____

_____

20_____

_____

_____

_____

_____

March 20

Are you a team player?

20_____

_____

_____

_____

_____

20_____

_____

_____

_____

_____

20_____

_____

_____

_____

_____

March 21

What made today special?

20_____

_____

_____

_____

_____

20_____

_____

_____

_____

20_____

_____

_____

_____

March 22

How do you develop self-esteem within students?

20_____

_____

_____

_____

_____

20_____

_____

_____

_____

_____

20_____

_____

_____

_____

_____

March 23

How do you prepare students for standardize testing?

20_____

_____

_____

_____

_____

20_____

_____

_____

_____

_____

20_____

_____

_____

_____

_____

March 24

Have you ever utilized a class newsletter? What did you include in the letter?

20_____

_____

_____

_____

_____

20_____

_____

_____

_____

_____

20_____

_____

_____

_____

_____

March 25

What course of action would you take if a student says he or she is being bullied?

20_____

_____

_____

_____

20_____

_____

_____

_____

20_____

_____

_____

_____

March 26

Name three times in the past where you overcame an obstacle or in which you achieved success.

20_____

_____

_____

_____

20_____

_____

_____

_____

20_____

_____

_____

_____

March 27

What do you do if the whole class is "not getting it"?

20_____

_____

_____

_____

_____

20_____

_____

_____

_____

_____

20_____

_____

_____

_____

_____

March 28

In what ways do you have students use higher-order thinking skills in the classroom?

20_____

_____

_____

_____

_____

20_____

_____

_____

_____

_____

20_____

_____

_____

_____

_____

March 29

What are your thoughts about homework?

20_____

_____

_____

_____

_____

20_____

_____

_____

_____

_____

20_____

_____

_____

_____

_____

March 30

What are some techniques you use to teach besides direct instruction?

20_____

_____

_____

_____

20_____

_____

_____

_____

20_____

_____

_____

_____

March 31

How do you communicate with parents on a regular basis?

20_____

_____

_____

_____

20_____

_____

_____

_____

20_____

_____

_____

_____

April 1

Is your work environment positive and supportive?

20_____

_____

_____

_____

_____

20_____

_____

_____

_____

_____

20_____

_____

_____

_____

_____

April 2

How would you respond if a parent complained about your class?

20_____

_____

_____

_____

20_____

_____

_____

_____

20_____

_____

_____

_____

April 3

How important is prioritizing your responsibilities?

20_____

_____

_____

_____

20_____

_____

_____

_____

20_____

_____

_____

_____

April 4

How do you accommodate for a gifted student in your class?

20_____

_____

_____

_____

_____

20_____

_____

_____

_____

_____

20_____

_____

_____

_____

_____

April 5

What are your weaknesses?

20_____

_____

_____

_____

_____

20_____

_____

_____

_____

_____

20_____

_____

_____

_____

_____

April 6

When are you most productive in your day?

20_____

_____

_____

_____

_____

20_____

_____

_____

_____

20_____

_____

_____

_____

April 7

Do you enjoy speaking in front of an audience?

20_____

_____

_____

_____

_____

20_____

_____

_____

_____

_____

20_____

_____

_____

_____

_____

April 8

Explain how you meet IEP needs.

20_____

_____

_____

_____

_____

20_____

_____

_____

_____

_____

20_____

_____

_____

_____

_____

April 9

What types of rewards best motivate you?

20_____

_____

_____

_____

_____

20_____

_____

_____

_____

_____

20_____

_____

_____

_____

_____

April 10

Give an example of effective communication with an administrator.

20_____

_____

_____

_____

20_____

_____

_____

_____

20_____

_____

_____

_____

April 11

How do you connect your lessons to the "real world"?

20_____

_____

_____

_____

_____

20_____

_____

_____

_____

_____

20_____

_____

_____

_____

April 12

How did you choose which college to attend?

20_____

_____

_____

_____

_____

20_____

_____

_____

_____

_____

20_____

_____

_____

_____

_____

April 13

What's the last thing you changed your mind about?

20_____

_____

_____

_____

_____

20_____

_____

_____

_____

_____

20_____

_____

_____

_____

_____

April 14

How do you keep parents aware of their son's or daughter's grades?

20_____

_____

_____

_____

20_____

_____

_____

_____

20_____

_____

_____

_____

April 15

What's the best advice you've ever received?

20_____

_____

_____

_____

_____

20_____

_____

_____

_____

_____

20_____

_____

_____

_____

_____

April 16

What areas of your life are working well for you?

20_____

_____

_____

_____

_____

20_____

_____

_____

_____

_____

20_____

_____

_____

_____

_____

April 17

Give an example of how you differentiated instruction in a lesson.

20_____

_____

_____

_____

_____

20_____

_____

_____

_____

20_____

_____

_____

_____

April 18

What skills or talents do you have that you are passionate about using?

20_____

_____

_____

_____

20_____

_____

_____

_____

20_____

_____

_____

_____

April 19

Consider a previous or current job- what specific activities have you done that you enjoy and find engaging?

20_____

_____

_____

_____

_____

20_____

_____

_____

_____

_____

20_____

_____

_____

_____

_____

April 20

What are your top five most prominent core values?

20_____

_____

_____

_____

_____

20_____

_____

_____

_____

_____

20_____

_____

_____

_____

_____

April 21

What do you do for creative expression?

20_____

_____

_____

_____

_____

20_____

_____

_____

_____

_____

20_____

_____

_____

_____

_____

April 22

How do you manage students with different reading abilities?

20_____

_____

_____

_____

_____

20_____

_____

_____

_____

_____

20_____

_____

_____

_____

_____

April 23

What do you put into the learning objectives of your lesson plans?

20_____

_____

_____

_____

20_____

_____

_____

_____

20_____

_____

_____

_____

April 24

What's your favorite go-to bellringer?

20_____

_____

_____

_____

20_____

_____

_____

_____

20_____

_____

_____

_____

April 25

Are you preparing for retirement?

20_____

_____

_____

_____

_____

20_____

_____

_____

_____

_____

20_____

_____

_____

_____

_____

April 26

Have you ever had to deal with any angry parent?

20_____

_____

_____

_____

_____

20_____

_____

_____

_____

_____

20_____

_____

_____

_____

_____

April 27

Do you use games to review your subject content?

20_____

_____

_____

_____

_____

20_____

_____

_____

_____

_____

20_____

_____

_____

_____

_____

April 28

During an average week, how much of your time is spent doing things you dislike or that you feel waste your time?

20_____

_____

_____

_____

20_____

_____

_____

_____

20_____

_____

_____

_____

April 29

How do you accommodate for non-English speakers?

20_____

_____

_____

_____

_____

20_____

_____

_____

_____

_____

20_____

_____

_____

_____

_____

April 30

What is your classroom management plan?

20_____

_____

_____

_____

_____

20_____

_____

_____

_____

_____

20_____

_____

_____

_____

_____

May 1

How do you spend your weekends?

20_____

_____

_____

_____

_____

20_____

_____

_____

_____

_____

20_____

_____

_____

_____

_____

May 2

What are your classroom rules?

20_____

_____

_____

_____

_____

20_____

_____

_____

_____

_____

20_____

_____

_____

_____

_____

May 3

How satisfied are you with your current work environment?

20_____

_____

_____

_____

20_____

_____

_____

_____

20_____

_____

_____

_____

May 4

How do you feel about inclusive classrooms?

20_____

_____

_____

_____

_____

20_____

_____

_____

_____

_____

20_____

_____

_____

_____

_____

May 5

Have you ever created a behavior modified plan for ongoing misbehavior?

20_____

_____

_____

_____

_____

20_____

_____

_____

_____

_____

20_____

_____

_____

_____

_____

May 6

What would you do if you caught a student cheating?

20_____

_____

_____

_____

_____

20_____

_____

_____

_____

_____

20_____

_____

_____

_____

_____

May 7

What's your favorite subject to talk about?

20_____

_____

_____

_____

_____

20_____

_____

_____

_____

_____

20_____

_____

_____

_____

_____

May 8

What do you want to accomplish today?

20_____

_____

_____

_____

_____

20_____

_____

_____

_____

20_____

_____

_____

_____

_____

May 9

Do you have any experience co-teaching with an inclusion specialist?

20_____

_____

_____

_____

_____

20_____

_____

_____

_____

20_____

_____

_____

_____

_____

May 10

What role does discipline play in teaching?

20_____

_____

_____

_____

_____

20_____

_____

_____

_____

_____

20_____

_____

_____

_____

_____

May 11

Describe a favorite holiday.

20_____

_____

_____

_____

_____

20_____

_____

_____

_____

_____

20_____

_____

_____

_____

_____

May 12

What characteristics do students want their teacher to possess?

20_____

_____

_____

_____

20_____

_____

_____

_____

20_____

_____

_____

_____

May 13

What do you wish you had spent less time worrying about?

20_____

_____

_____

_____

20_____

_____

_____

_____

20_____

_____

_____

_____

May 14

How does a teacher's attitude affect his/her success?

20_____

_____

_____

_____

_____

20_____

_____

_____

_____

20_____

_____

_____

_____

_____

May 15

Do you need an alarm clock to wake up in the morning?

20_____

_____

_____

_____

_____

20_____

_____

_____

_____

_____

20_____

_____

_____

_____

_____

May 16

How would your past students describe you?

20_____

_____

_____

_____

_____

20_____

_____

_____

_____

_____

20_____

_____

_____

_____

_____

May 17

Does your life and work currently reflect your values?

20_____

_____

_____

_____

_____

20_____

_____

_____

_____

_____

20_____

_____

_____

_____

_____

May 18

What is your educational background?

20_____

_____

_____

_____

20_____

_____

_____

_____

20_____

_____

_____

_____

May 19

What teams or extracurricular activities did you participate in during school?

20_____

_____

_____

_____

_____

20_____

_____

_____

_____

_____

20_____

_____

_____

_____

_____

May 20

What is the last book you've read?

20_____

_____

_____

_____

_____

20_____

_____

_____

_____

20_____

_____

_____

_____

May 21

What do you dislike most about teaching?

20_____

_____

_____

_____

_____

20_____

_____

_____

_____

20_____

_____

_____

_____

May 22

What activities are your biggest time wasters?

20_____

_____

_____

_____

_____

20_____

_____

_____

_____

_____

20_____

_____

_____

_____

_____

May 23

Describe your teaching style.

20_____

_____

_____

_____

_____

20_____

_____

_____

_____

_____

20_____

_____

_____

_____

_____

May 24

What was your last vacation?

20_____

_____

_____

_____

_____

20_____

_____

_____

_____

_____

20_____

_____

_____

_____

_____

May 25

What is the greatest challenge facing teachers today?

20_____

_____

_____

_____

_____

20_____

_____

_____

_____

_____

20_____

_____

_____

_____

_____

May 26

How do you handle stress?

20_____

_____

_____

_____

_____

20_____

_____

_____

_____

_____

20_____

_____

_____

_____

_____

May 27

Describe your worst teaching day.

20_____

_____

_____

_____

_____

20_____

_____

_____

_____

_____

20_____

_____

_____

_____

_____

May 28

Describe a troubling student you've taught and what you've done to get through to him/her.

20_____

_____

_____

_____

_____

20_____

_____

_____

_____

20_____

_____

_____

_____

_____

May 29

What was the last compliment someone gave you? What was the last compliment you gave someone else?

20_____

_____

_____

_____

_____

20_____

_____

_____

_____

_____

20_____

_____

_____

_____

_____

May 30

Name one item you can't throw away.

20_____

_____

_____

_____

_____

20_____

_____

_____

_____

_____

20_____

_____

_____

_____

_____

May 31

Describe your professional development experience.

20_____

_____

_____

_____

_____

20_____

_____

_____

_____

_____

20_____

_____

_____

_____

_____

June 1

How important are strong working relationships to you?

20_____

_____

_____

_____

_____

20_____

_____

_____

_____

20_____

_____

_____

_____

June 2

How do you approach different learning styles?

20_____

_____

_____

_____

_____

20_____

_____

_____

_____

_____

20_____

_____

_____

_____

_____

June 3

How important is dealing with discipline issues promptly to you?

20_____

_____

_____

_____

_____

20_____

_____

_____

_____

_____

20_____

_____

_____

_____

_____

June 4

How fulfilled are you with the way in which you're currently living your life?

20_____

_____

_____

_____

_____

20_____

_____

_____

_____

_____

20_____

_____

_____

_____

_____

June 5

What makes you different from other people?

20_____

_____

_____

_____

_____

20_____

_____

_____

_____

20_____

_____

_____

_____

June 6

How do you feel around negative people?

20_____

_____

_____

_____

_____

20_____

_____

_____

_____

_____

20_____

_____

_____

_____

_____

June 7

How do you encourage students to express their creativity?

20_____

_____

_____

_____

20_____

_____

_____

_____

20_____

_____

_____

_____

June 8

How do you approach a student that refuses to participate?

20_____

_____

_____

_____

_____

20_____

_____

_____

_____

_____

20_____

_____

_____

_____

_____

June 9

Under what circumstances do you ever find yourself angry?

20_____

_____

_____

_____

20_____

_____

_____

_____

20_____

_____

_____

_____

June 10

How do you leverage resources in the community to enhance your teaching?

20_____

_____

_____

_____

_____

20_____

_____

_____

_____

_____

20_____

_____

_____

_____

_____

June 11

What could a visitor to your classroom expect to see?

20_____

_____

_____

_____

_____

20_____

_____

_____

_____

_____

20_____

_____

_____

_____

_____

June 12

Did you have a favorite teacher?

20_____

_____

_____

_____

_____

20_____

_____

_____

_____

_____

20_____

_____

_____

_____

_____

June 13

If the majority of your class failed a test, what would you do?

20_____

_____

_____

_____

20_____

_____

_____

_____

20_____

_____

_____

_____

_____

June 14

What would you like your students to take from their learning experience with you?

20_____

_____

_____

_____

_____

20_____

_____

_____

_____

_____

20_____

_____

_____

_____

_____

June 15

How do you use data to differentiate instruction and support students?

20_____

_____

_____

_____

20_____

_____

_____

_____

20_____

_____

_____

_____

June 16

How do you support literacy for all students?

20_____

_____

_____

_____

_____

20_____

_____

_____

_____

_____

20_____

_____

_____

_____

_____

June 17

Do you incorporate collaborative and project-based learning in your lesson plans?

20_____

_____

_____

_____

20_____

_____

_____

_____

20_____

_____

_____

_____

June 18

How do you promote student voice and choice to help them become self-directed learners?

20_____

_____

_____

_____

_____

20_____

_____

_____

_____

_____

20_____

_____

_____

_____

_____

June 19

How do you guide students to be global citizens?

20_____

_____

_____

_____

_____

20_____

_____

_____

_____

20_____

_____

_____

_____

June 20

How many unopened emails do you have?

20_____

_____

_____

_____

_____

20_____

_____

_____

_____

_____

20_____

_____

_____

_____

_____

June 21

What are some of your most successful classroom management techniques?

20_____

_____

_____

_____

20_____

_____

_____

_____

20_____

_____

_____

_____

June 22

Do you handle a difficult/demanding parent?

20_____

_____

_____

_____

_____

20_____

_____

_____

_____

_____

20_____

_____

_____

_____

_____

June 23

How do you feel about evaluations?

20_____

_____

_____

_____

_____

20_____

_____

_____

_____

_____

20_____

_____

_____

_____

_____

June 24

Describe the last professional development book or training that improved your teaching.

20_____

_____

_____

_____

_____

20_____

_____

_____

_____

_____

20_____

_____

_____

_____

_____

June 25

What are some ways you build relationships with your students?

20_____

_____

_____

_____

20_____

_____

_____

_____

20_____

_____

_____

_____

_____

June 26

What are your favorite shoes?

20_____

_____

_____

_____

_____

20_____

_____

_____

_____

_____

20_____

_____

_____

_____

_____

June 27

What are, in your opinion, the most important skills for teachers? Name three of them.

20_____

_____

_____

_____

20_____

_____

_____

_____

20_____

_____

_____

_____

_____

June 28

How do you motivate students to learn?

20_____

_____

_____

_____

_____

20_____

_____

_____

_____

20_____

_____

_____

_____

June 29

How do you evaluate your students?

20_____

_____

_____

_____

_____

20_____

_____

_____

_____

20_____

_____

_____

_____

June 30

Do you have a unique talent?

20_____

_____

_____

_____

_____

20_____

_____

_____

_____

_____

20_____

_____

_____

_____

_____

July 1

What teaching resources do you use in your lessons?

20_____

_____

_____

_____

_____

20_____

_____

_____

_____

_____

20_____

_____

_____

_____

_____

July 2

What do you say to students on the first day?

20_____

_____

_____

_____

_____

20_____

_____

_____

_____

_____

20_____

_____

_____

_____

July 3

What additional classes or training have you attended?

20_____

_____

_____

_____

20_____

_____

_____

_____

20_____

_____

_____

_____

July 4

How do you incorporate SEL (Social Emotional Learning) into your lessons?

20_____

_____

_____

_____

_____

20_____

_____

_____

_____

_____

20_____

_____

_____

_____

_____

July 5

If you were on a sports team, what contribution would you make?

20_____

_____

_____

_____

20_____

_____

_____

_____

20_____

_____

_____

_____

July 6

What motivates you?

20_____

_____

_____

_____

_____

20_____

_____

_____

_____

_____

20_____

_____

_____

_____

_____

July 7

What's your preferred style of communication: verbal or nonverbal?

20_____

_____

_____

_____

20_____

_____

_____

_____

20_____

_____

_____

_____

July 8

Do you reward yourself when you accomplish tasks?

20_____

_____

_____

_____

_____

20_____

_____

_____

_____

_____

20_____

_____

_____

_____

_____

July 9

What results would you like to achieve?

20_____

_____

_____

_____

_____

20_____

_____

_____

_____

_____

20_____

_____

_____

_____

July 10

How do you handle a student that is habitually late?

20_____

_____

_____

_____

_____

20_____

_____

_____

_____

_____

20_____

_____

_____

_____

_____

July 11

Have you ever taken students on a field trip?

20_____

_____

_____

_____

_____

20_____

_____

_____

_____

_____

20_____

_____

_____

_____

_____

July 12

In your opinion, what is something a teacher should never say to students?

20_____

_____

_____

_____

_____

20_____

_____

_____

_____

_____

20_____

_____

_____

_____

_____

July 13

What is a typical workday look like?

20_____
_____
_____
_____
_____

20_____
_____
_____
_____
_____

20_____
_____
_____
_____
_____

July 14

What's a funny story people tell about you?

20_____

_____

_____

_____

_____

20_____

_____

_____

_____

_____

20_____

_____

_____

_____

_____

July 15

What is a problem you solved today?

20_____

_____

_____

_____

_____

20_____

_____

_____

_____

_____

20_____

_____

_____

_____

_____

July 16

How do you measure success?

20_____

_____

_____

_____

_____

20_____

_____

_____

_____

_____

20_____

_____

_____

_____

_____

July 17

Who do you work most closely with?

20_____

_____

_____

_____

_____

20_____

_____

_____

_____

_____

20_____

_____

_____

_____

_____

July 18

How do you handle student feedback?

20_____

_____

_____

_____

20_____

_____

_____

_____

20_____

_____

_____

_____

July 19

What special benefits or perks come with your job?

20_____

_____

_____

_____

_____

20_____

_____

_____

_____

_____

20_____

_____

_____

_____

_____

July 20

What do you think can negatively affect a student's performance at school, aside from bad friends and depression?

20_____

_____

_____

_____

_____

20_____

_____

_____

_____

_____

20_____

_____

_____

_____

_____

July 21

How would you describe the importance of physical exercise?

20_____

_____

_____

_____

_____

20_____

_____

_____

_____

_____

20_____

_____

_____

_____

_____

July 22

When's the last time you had a belly laugh?

20_____

_____

_____

_____

_____

20_____

_____

_____

_____

_____

20_____

_____

_____

_____

_____

July 23

What do you think parents can do for their students at home to improve their learning ability?

20_____

_____

_____

_____

20_____

_____

_____

_____

20_____

_____

_____

_____

_____

July 24

Do you have a favorite quote?

20_____

_____

_____

_____

_____

20_____

_____

_____

_____

_____

20_____

_____

_____

_____

_____

July 25

What's the craziest excuse you've heard from a student?

20_____

_____

_____

_____

_____

20_____

_____

_____

_____

_____

20_____

_____

_____

_____

_____

July 26

What do you consider to be your biggest achievement?

20_____

_____

_____

_____

_____

20_____

_____

_____

_____

_____

20_____

_____

_____

_____

_____

Jul 27

Do you wear a watch?

20_____

_____

_____

_____

20_____

_____

_____

_____

20_____

_____

_____

_____

July 28

What do you think the first thing a student should do when he or she gets home?

20_____

_____

_____

_____

_____

20_____

_____

_____

_____

_____

20_____

_____

_____

_____

_____

July 29

What are the key elements for smooth classroom learning and discussion?

20_____

_____

_____

_____

20_____

_____

_____

_____

20_____

_____

_____

_____

July 30

What's the worst behavior you have ever seen a student exhibit in the classroom?

20_____

_____

_____

_____

_____

20_____

_____

_____

_____

_____

20_____

_____

_____

_____

_____

July 31

What's the last museum you visited?

20_____

_____

_____

_____

_____

20_____

_____

_____

_____

20_____

_____

_____

_____

August 1

Do you have a healthy and rewarding work/life balance?

20_____

_____

_____

_____

_____

20_____

_____

_____

_____

_____

20_____

_____

_____

_____

_____

August 2

How important is establishing personal and professional boundaries to you?

20_____

_____

_____

_____

_____

20_____

_____

_____

_____

_____

20_____

_____

_____

_____

_____

August 3

What's that 'thing' students often learn after it's too late?

20_____

_____

_____

_____

_____

20_____

_____

_____

_____

_____

20_____

_____

_____

_____

_____

August 4

What's your favorite movie for students?

20_____

_____

_____

_____

_____

20_____

_____

_____

_____

_____

20_____

_____

_____

_____

_____

August 5

Would you ever break any of the teaching ethics to help a student battling with depression?

20_____

_____

_____

_____

_____

20_____

_____

_____

_____

_____

20_____

_____

_____

_____

_____

August 6

What keeps you going?

20_____

_____

_____

_____

_____

20_____

_____

_____

_____

20_____

_____

_____

_____

August 7

Are you a good listener?

20_____

_____

_____

_____

_____

20_____

_____

_____

_____

20_____

_____

_____

_____

August 8

What is your normal work week?

20_____

_____

_____

_____

_____

20_____

_____

_____

_____

_____

20_____

_____

_____

_____

_____

August 9

How would you describe your elementary school experience?

20_____

_____

_____

_____

_____

20_____

_____

_____

_____

_____

20_____

_____

_____

_____

_____

August 10

Where's your favorite place that you would love to take
your students?

20_____

_____

_____

_____

20_____

_____

_____

_____

20_____

_____

_____

_____

August 11

What do you miss most about being a child?

20_____

_____

_____

_____

_____

20_____

_____

_____

_____

_____

20_____

_____

_____

_____

_____

August 12

What's the worst thing you did as a student? Do you regret it?

20_____

_____

_____

_____

20_____

_____

_____

_____

20_____

_____

_____

_____

August 13

What is your favorite snack?

20_____

_____

_____

_____

_____

20_____

_____

_____

_____

_____

20_____

_____

_____

_____

_____

August 14

What bothered you today?

20_____

_____

_____

_____

20_____

_____

_____

_____

20_____

_____

_____

_____

August 15

Is teaching your dream job?

20_____

_____

_____

_____

_____

20_____

_____

_____

_____

_____

20_____

_____

_____

_____

_____

August 16

How ambitious do you feel today?

20_____

_____

_____

_____

_____

20_____

_____

_____

_____

20_____

_____

_____

_____

August 17

What details from today would you like to remember?

20_____

_____

_____

_____

_____

20_____

_____

_____

_____

_____

20_____

_____

_____

_____

_____

August 18

What do you do when a student asks a question that you don't know the answer?

20_____

_____

_____

_____

20_____

_____

_____

_____

20_____

_____

_____

_____

_____

August 19

What advice would you give to a school dropout?

20_____

_____

_____

_____

_____

20_____

_____

_____

_____

_____

20_____

_____

_____

_____

_____

August 20

On a scale of one to ten, how spontaneous were you today?

20_____

_____

_____

_____

20_____

_____

_____

_____

20_____

_____

_____

_____

August 21

What's your favorite outfit?

20_____

_____

_____

_____

_____

20_____

_____

_____

_____

_____

20_____

_____

_____

_____

_____

August 22

What's your favorite comfort food?

20_____

_____

_____

_____

_____

20_____

_____

_____

_____

_____

20_____

_____

_____

_____

_____

August 23

Have you ever been on television or the radio?

20_____

_____

_____

_____

_____

20_____

_____

_____

_____

_____

20_____

_____

_____

_____

_____

August 24

If you could make a new law to govern all students in schools, what law would you make?

20_____

_____

_____

_____

20_____

_____

_____

_____

20_____

_____

_____

_____

_____

August 25

What plan can you make to spruce up your workspace to make it feel more joyful?

20_____

_____

_____

_____

_____

20_____

_____

_____

_____

_____

20_____

_____

_____

_____

_____

August 26

What's an ideal reading/studying environment like?

20_____

_____

_____

_____

_____

20_____

_____

_____

_____

_____

20_____

_____

_____

_____

_____

August 27

What countries have you traveled to?

20_____

_____

_____

_____

_____

20_____

_____

_____

_____

_____

20_____

_____

_____

_____

_____

August 28

What's something interesting about you that most people may not know?

20_____

_____

_____

_____

20_____

_____

_____

_____

20_____

_____

_____

_____

August 29

What's been one of your biggest challenges?

20_____

_____

_____

_____

_____

20_____

_____

_____

_____

_____

20_____

_____

_____

_____

_____

August 30

Who/what inspired you to be a teacher?

20_____

_____

_____

_____

_____

20_____

_____

_____

_____

20_____

_____

_____

_____

August 31

What's a life lesson that's benefitted you?

20_____

_____

_____

_____

_____

20_____

_____

_____

_____

_____

20_____

_____

_____

_____

_____

September 1

Does your career stimulate and develop you as a
person?

20_____

_____

_____

_____

_____

20_____

_____

_____

_____

_____

20_____

_____

_____

_____

_____

September 2

What do you think is preventing students from studying hard?

20_____

_____

_____

_____

_____

20_____

_____

_____

_____

_____

20_____

_____

_____

_____

_____

September 3

Have you ever used foul language in front of a student?

20_____

_____

_____

_____

_____

20_____

_____

_____

_____

20_____

_____

_____

_____

September 4

Can you predict student performance on exams by merely looking at his/her performance in the classroom?

20_____

_____

_____

_____

20_____

_____

_____

_____

20_____

_____

_____

_____

September 5

What's the most disgusting thing a student has ever done in your classroom?

20_____

_____

_____

_____

_____

20_____

_____

_____

_____

_____

20_____

_____

_____

_____

_____

September 6

How strict were your parents towards education?

20_____

_____

_____

_____

_____

20_____

_____

_____

_____

_____

20_____

_____

_____

_____

_____

September 7

What was the most difficult class you ever attended?

20_____

_____

_____

_____

_____

20_____

_____

_____

_____

_____

20_____

_____

_____

_____

_____

September 8

What's the most overrated piece of equipment in school?

20_____

_____

_____

_____

_____

20_____

_____

_____

_____

_____

20_____

_____

_____

_____

_____

September 9

Do you handle rejection well?

20_____

_____

_____

_____

_____

20_____

_____

_____

_____

_____

20_____

_____

_____

_____

_____

September 10

What is the best way to resolve a fight between students?

20_____

_____

_____

_____

_____

20_____

_____

_____

_____

_____

20_____

_____

_____

_____

_____

September 11

Where were you during 9/11? What do you remember?

20_____

_____

_____

_____

_____

20_____

_____

_____

_____

_____

20_____

_____

_____

_____

_____

September 12

What would your advice be to a student wanting to get a boyfriend or girlfriend if he or she wants?

20_____

_____

_____

_____

_____

20_____

_____

_____

_____

_____

20_____

_____

_____

_____

_____

September 13

Describe a cherished memory.

20_____

_____

_____

_____

_____

20_____

_____

_____

_____

_____

20_____

_____

_____

_____

_____

September 14

What is the best piece of advice you've received from a student?

20_____

_____

_____

_____

20_____

_____

_____

_____

20_____

_____

_____

_____

September 15

How could today have been better?

20_____

_____

_____

_____

_____

20_____

_____

_____

_____

_____

20_____

_____

_____

_____

_____

September 16

What's your favorite outdoor activity?

20_____

_____

_____

_____

_____

20_____

_____

_____

_____

_____

20_____

_____

_____

_____

_____

September 17

Who was your worst teacher in school? Why?

20_____

_____

_____

_____

_____

20_____

_____

_____

_____

_____

20_____

_____

_____

_____

_____

September 18

What's on your to-do list?

20_____

_____

_____

_____

_____

20_____

_____

_____

_____

_____

20_____

_____

_____

_____

_____

September 19

How do you practice self-care?

20_____

_____

_____

_____

20_____

_____

_____

_____

20_____

_____

_____

_____

September 20

What's the funniest thing you've seen a student do?

20_____

_____

_____

_____

_____

20_____

_____

_____

_____

_____

20_____

_____

_____

_____

_____

September 21

What do you try to avoid?

20_____

_____

_____

_____

_____

20_____

_____

_____

_____

20_____

_____

_____

_____

September 22

What do you love about your life?

20_____

_____

_____

_____

_____

20_____

_____

_____

_____

_____

20_____

_____

_____

_____

_____

September 23

What did you get done today?

20_____

_____

_____

_____

_____

20_____

_____

_____

_____

_____

20_____

_____

_____

_____

_____

September 24

What is your personal motto?

20_____

_____

_____

_____

_____

20_____

_____

_____

_____

_____

20_____

_____

_____

_____

_____

September 25

What's that one thing that students don't believe about you when you tell them?

20_____

_____

_____

_____

_____

20_____

_____

_____

_____

_____

20_____

_____

_____

_____

_____

September 26

What about your lessons could you improve?

20_____

_____

_____

_____

_____

20_____

_____

_____

_____

_____

20_____

_____

_____

_____

September 27

What's unique about you?

20_____

_____

_____

_____

_____

20_____

_____

_____

_____

_____

20_____

_____

_____

_____

_____

September 28

List three things that made you smile today.

20_____

_____

_____

_____

_____

20_____

_____

_____

_____

_____

20_____

_____

_____

_____

_____

September 29

How do you stay organized?

20_____

_____

_____

_____

_____

20_____

_____

_____

_____

20_____

_____

_____

_____

September 30

What is one positive change you have already made this year?

20_____

_____

_____

_____

_____

20_____

_____

_____

_____

_____

20_____

_____

_____

_____

_____

October 1

How much do you look forward to going to work each day?

20_____

_____

_____

_____

20_____

_____

_____

_____

20_____

_____

_____

_____

October 2

How happy are you with your current job performance?

20_____

_____

_____

_____

_____

20_____

_____

_____

_____

_____

20_____

_____

_____

_____

_____

October 3

How do you spend your summer breaks?

20_____

_____

_____

_____

_____

20_____

_____

_____

_____

_____

20_____

_____

_____

_____

_____

October 4

What are the main challenges (or difficulties) that you're currently facing in life?

20_____

_____

_____

_____

_____

20_____

_____

_____

_____

_____

20_____

_____

_____

_____

_____

October 5

If you won the lottery, would you give up teaching? What would you do instead?

20_____

_____

_____

_____

20_____

_____

_____

_____

20_____

_____

_____

_____

October 6

What are some traditions or superstitions you have about the first day of school?

20_____

_____

_____

_____

20_____

_____

_____

_____

20_____

_____

_____

_____

October 7

What's your most embarrassing teaching moment?

20_____

_____

_____

_____

_____

20_____

_____

_____

_____

_____

20_____

_____

_____

_____

_____

October 8

How well do you focus at work?

20_____

_____

_____

_____

_____

20_____

_____

_____

_____

_____

20_____

_____

_____

_____

_____

October 9

What current trends are baffling you? Why?

20_____

_____

_____

_____

_____

20_____

_____

_____

_____

_____

20_____

_____

_____

_____

_____

October 10

What differences have you observed between the morning students and afternoon classes?

20_____

_____

_____

_____

20_____

_____

_____

_____

20_____

_____

_____

_____

October 11

What's the strangest thing that has ever happened to you?

20_____

_____

_____

_____

20_____

_____

_____

_____

20_____

_____

_____

_____

October 12

If you could share one piece of wisdom with your students, what would it be?

20_____

_____

_____

_____

_____

20_____

_____

_____

_____

_____

20_____

_____

_____

_____

_____

October 13

What are you most proud of?

20_____

_____

_____

_____

20_____

_____

_____

_____

20_____

_____

_____

_____

October 14

How do you remember all of your students' names? How long does it take you?

20_____

_____

_____

_____

_____

20_____

_____

_____

_____

_____

20_____

_____

_____

_____

_____

October 15

How did you send your day?

20_____

_____

_____

_____

_____

20_____

_____

_____

_____

_____

20_____

_____

_____

_____

_____

October 16

If you could have a superpower just for today, what would it be?

20_____

_____

_____

_____

_____

20_____

_____

_____

_____

20_____

_____

_____

_____

_____

October 17

What's your favorite thing to do on a rainy day?

20_____

_____

_____

_____

_____

20_____

_____

_____

_____

20_____

_____

_____

_____

October 18

What was in your mailbox today?

20_____

_____

_____

_____

_____

20_____

_____

_____

_____

_____

20_____

_____

_____

_____

_____

October 19

Why do (or don't) you friend former students on Facebook?

20_____

_____

_____

_____

20_____

_____

_____

_____

20_____

_____

_____

_____

October 20

What is a decision you made today?

20_____

_____

_____

_____

_____

20_____

_____

_____

_____

_____

20_____

_____

_____

_____

October 21

If you were given a superlative, what would it be?

20_____

_____

_____

_____

_____

20_____

_____

_____

_____

_____

20_____

_____

_____

_____

_____

October 22

What is the most important thing you should
accomplish in the next 24 hours?

20_____

_____

_____

_____

_____

20_____

_____

_____

_____

_____

20_____

_____

_____

_____

_____

October 23

What was a difficult situation you handled? What did you do? What were the results?

20_____

_____

_____

_____

_____

20_____

_____

_____

_____

_____

20_____

_____

_____

_____

_____

October 24

What new activity have you tried?

20_____

_____

_____

_____

20_____

_____

_____

_____

20_____

_____

_____

_____

October 25

How do you want to be remembered?

20_____

_____

_____

_____

_____

20_____

_____

_____

_____

_____

20_____

_____

_____

_____

_____

October 26

If you could change one thing about today, what would it be?

20_____

_____

_____

_____

20_____

_____

_____

_____

20_____

_____

_____

_____

October 27

How do you take a difficult task and make it fun and exciting?

20_____

_____

_____

_____

_____

20_____

_____

_____

_____

20_____

_____

_____

_____

_____

October 28

What question(s) do you hate to answer?

20_____

_____

_____

_____

_____

20_____

_____

_____

_____

_____

20_____

_____

_____

_____

_____

October 29

What kinds of opportunities do you give students to teach each other?

20_____

_____

_____

_____

20_____

_____

_____

_____

20_____

_____

_____

_____

October 30

In three words, describe your day.

20_____

_____

_____

_____

_____

20_____

_____

_____

_____

_____

20_____

_____

_____

_____

_____

October 31

What could you talk about for 60 minutes without preparation?

20_____

_____

_____

_____

20_____

_____

_____

_____

20_____

_____

_____

_____

November 1

How fulfilled are you in your current work environment?

20_____

_____

_____

_____

_____

20_____

_____

_____

_____

_____

20_____

_____

_____

_____

_____

November 2

How content are you with the amount of free time you have?

20_____

_____

_____

_____

_____

20_____

_____

_____

_____

_____

20_____

_____

_____

_____

_____

November 3

How do you regularly make a positive impact in the lives of other people?

20_____

_____

_____

_____

_____

20_____

_____

_____

_____

_____

20_____

_____

_____

_____

_____

November 4

What is working really well in your life at this stage of your life?

20_____

_____

_____

_____

20_____

_____

_____

_____

20_____

_____

_____

_____

November 5

Who is the kindest student you have in class?

20_____

_____

_____

_____

_____

20_____

_____

_____

_____

_____

20_____

_____

_____

_____

_____

November 6

How do you get your students to follow directions?

20_____

_____

_____

_____

20_____

_____

_____

_____

20_____

_____

_____

_____

November 7

How do you answer students when they ask "Are we doing anything today?"

20_____

_____

_____

_____

20_____

_____

_____

_____

20_____

_____

_____

_____

November 8

Do you have any unfinished tasks/projects?

20_____

_____

_____

_____

_____

20_____

_____

_____

_____

_____

20_____

_____

_____

_____

_____

November 9

What's a lesson you learned this week?

20_____

_____

_____

_____

_____

20_____

_____

_____

_____

_____

20_____

_____

_____

_____

_____

November 10

What qualities do you most value in a colleague?

20_____

_____

_____

_____

_____

20_____

_____

_____

_____

_____

20_____

_____

_____

_____

_____

November 11

Do you count off for spelling?

20_____

_____

_____

_____

_____

20_____

_____

_____

_____

_____

20_____

_____

_____

_____

November 12

Who is the wisest person you know?

20_____

_____

_____

_____

20_____

_____

_____

_____

20_____

_____

_____

_____

November 13

Do you have any memorable stories about students?

20_____

_____

_____

_____

_____

20_____

_____

_____

_____

_____

20_____

_____

_____

_____

_____

November 14

How do you answer students when they ask "Do we need to know this?"

20_____

_____

_____

_____

_____

20_____

_____

_____

_____

_____

20_____

_____

_____

_____

_____

November 15

Do you offer extra credit?

20_____

_____

_____

_____

_____

20_____

_____

_____

_____

_____

20_____

_____

_____

_____

_____

November 16

What kind of information would you want to know about every student in your class?

20_____

_____

_____

_____

_____

20_____

_____

_____

_____

_____

20_____

_____

_____

_____

_____

November 17

How do you stay updated about the best practices in teaching?

20_____

_____

_____

_____

_____

20_____

_____

_____

_____

20_____

_____

_____

_____

_____

November 18

What is something you have that has improved the quality of your life?

20_____

_____

_____

_____

_____

20_____

_____

_____

_____

20_____

_____

_____

_____

_____

November 19

How would you recommend parents and student prepare for a new school year?

20_____

_____

_____

_____

_____

20_____

_____

_____

_____

_____

20_____

_____

_____

_____

_____

November 20

How do you show others that you appreciate them?

20_____

_____

_____

_____

_____

20_____

_____

_____

_____

_____

20_____

_____

_____

_____

_____

November 21

How do you make sure no student is left behind?

20_____

_____

_____

_____

_____

20_____

_____

_____

_____

_____

20_____

_____

_____

_____

_____

November 22

How do you promote overall hygiene among your learners?

20_____

_____

_____

_____

20_____

_____

_____

_____

20_____

_____

_____

_____

November 23

Have you had a student fall ill or get injured in your classroom? How did you respond?

20_____

_____

_____

_____

_____

20_____

_____

_____

_____

_____

20_____

_____

_____

_____

_____

November 24

How do you prioritize your time?

20_____

_____

_____

_____

_____

20_____

_____

_____

_____

_____

20_____

_____

_____

_____

_____

November 25

What three skills would you hope your students master before the end of the year?

20_____

_____

_____

_____

_____

20_____

_____

_____

_____

_____

20_____

_____

_____

_____

_____

November 26

What are you grateful for today?

20_____

_____

_____

_____

_____

20_____

_____

_____

_____

_____

20_____

_____

_____

_____

_____

November 27

When is the last time you had an inspiring conversation?

20_____

_____

_____

_____

_____

20_____

_____

_____

_____

_____

20_____

_____

_____

_____

_____

November 28

What verb best describes your day?

20_____

_____

_____

_____

_____

20_____

_____

_____

_____

_____

20_____

_____

_____

_____

_____

November 29

If you could send a message to a large group of people, who would those people be? What would be your message?

20_____

_____

_____

_____

_____

20_____

_____

_____

_____

_____

20_____

_____

_____

_____

_____

November 30

What job other than your own would you like to have?

20_____

_____

_____

_____

20_____

_____

_____

_____

20_____

_____

_____

_____

December 1

How satisfying are your career achievements to date?

20_____

_____

_____

_____

_____

20_____

_____

_____

_____

_____

20_____

_____

_____

_____

_____

December 2

If you could make a documentary about anything, what would you make it about?

20_____

_____

_____

_____

_____

20_____

_____

_____

_____

_____

20_____

_____

_____

_____

_____

December 3

You're on an elevator with your hero. You have 90 seconds to tell them about yourself. What do you say?

20_____

_____

_____

_____

_____

20_____

_____

_____

_____

_____

20_____

_____

_____

_____

_____

December 4

What do you geek out about?

20_____

_____

_____

_____

_____

20_____

_____

_____

_____

_____

20_____

_____

_____

_____

_____

December 5

What expectations do you have for yourself and your life?

20_____

_____

_____

_____

_____

20_____

_____

_____

_____

20_____

_____

_____

_____

_____

December 6

What is your attention on today?

20_____

_____

_____

_____

20_____

_____

_____

_____

20_____

_____

_____

_____

December 7

How do you see the people you work with? How do they see you?

20_____

_____

_____

_____

_____

20_____

_____

_____

_____

_____

20_____

_____

_____

_____

_____

December 8

What are three words to describe your social life?

20_____

_____

_____

_____

_____

20_____

_____

_____

_____

_____

20_____

_____

_____

_____

_____

December 9

What personal and professional goals do you want to
set for the coming new year?

20_____

_____

_____

_____

_____

20_____

_____

_____

_____

_____

20_____

_____

_____

_____

_____

December 10

What was the best part of your day?

20_____

_____

_____

_____

_____

20_____

_____

_____

_____

_____

20_____

_____

_____

_____

_____

December 11

If you had no deadlines, what project or task would you concentrate on right now?

20_____

_____

_____

_____

20_____

_____

_____

_____

20_____

_____

_____

_____

December 12

What is something that most people would be surprised to know about you?

20_____

_____

_____

_____

_____

20_____

_____

_____

_____

_____

20_____

_____

_____

_____

_____

December 13

What is something unusual that you own?

20_____

_____

_____

_____

_____

20_____

_____

_____

_____

_____

20_____

_____

_____

_____

_____

December 14

Where do you go for good ideas?

20_____

_____

_____

_____

_____

20_____

_____

_____

_____

_____

20_____

_____

_____

_____

_____

December 15

What's the last item you purchased for your classroom?

20_____

_____

_____

_____

_____

20_____

_____

_____

_____

_____

20_____

_____

_____

_____

_____

December 16

What technology do you use on a regular basis?

20_____

_____

_____

_____

_____

20_____

_____

_____

_____

_____

20_____

_____

_____

_____

_____

December 17

Where do you see yourself in five years?

20_____

_____

_____

_____

_____

20_____

_____

_____

_____

_____

20_____

_____

_____

_____

_____

December 18

What's the last check you wrote?

20_____

_____

_____

_____

_____

20_____

_____

_____

_____

20_____

_____

_____

_____

December 19

What advice would you give yourself three years ago?

20_____

_____

_____

_____

_____

20_____

_____

_____

_____

_____

20_____

_____

_____

_____

_____

December 20

Are you a risk taker? What's the last risk you took?

20_____

_____

_____

_____

_____

20_____

_____

_____

_____

_____

20_____

_____

_____

_____

_____

December 21

If you could trade jobs with someone for a day, who would you trade with and why?

20_____

_____

_____

_____

_____

20_____

_____

_____

_____

_____

20_____

_____

_____

_____

_____

December 22

When's the last time you had your haircut?

20_____

_____

_____

_____

_____

20_____

_____

_____

_____

_____

20_____

_____

_____

_____

_____

December 24

How are you spending your Winter Break?

20_____

_____

_____

_____

_____

20_____

_____

_____

_____

_____

20_____

_____

_____

_____

_____

December 25

What did you want to be when you were a child?

20_____

_____

_____

_____

_____

20_____

_____

_____

_____

_____

20_____

_____

_____

_____

_____

December 26

What's one word that captures how you want to feel next year? Why?

20_____

_____

_____

_____

_____

20_____

_____

_____

_____

_____

20_____

_____

_____

_____

_____

December 27

If you were to go back to school, what would you study?

20_____

_____

_____

_____

_____

20_____

_____

_____

_____

_____

20_____

_____

_____

_____

_____

December 28

How did you spend your day?

20_____

_____

_____

_____

_____

20_____

_____

_____

_____

_____

20_____

_____

_____

_____

_____

December 29

What do you love to learn about?

20_____

_____

_____

_____

_____

20_____

_____

_____

_____

_____

20_____

_____

_____

_____

_____

December 30

Write a phrase to describe your year.

20_____

_____

_____

_____

_____

20_____

_____

_____

_____

_____

20_____

_____

_____

_____

_____

December 31

What is your most cherished memory of this year?

20_____

_____

_____

_____

20_____

_____

_____

_____

20_____

_____

_____

_____